MARIE'S OCEAN

MARIE THARP MAPS THE MOUNTAINS UNDER THE SEA

Josie James

Christy Ottaviano Books

Henry Holt and Company

New York

For my parents, Josephine and James Adinolfi.
For all great people whose names we do not know.

I would like to extend my gratitude to my STEM hero, Dr. Julie Bryce,
Professor of Geochemistry at the University of New Hampshire, for taking the time
to review my work even while on her way to do research in the Arctic.

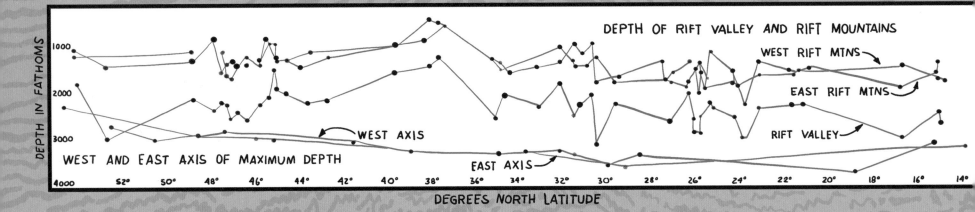

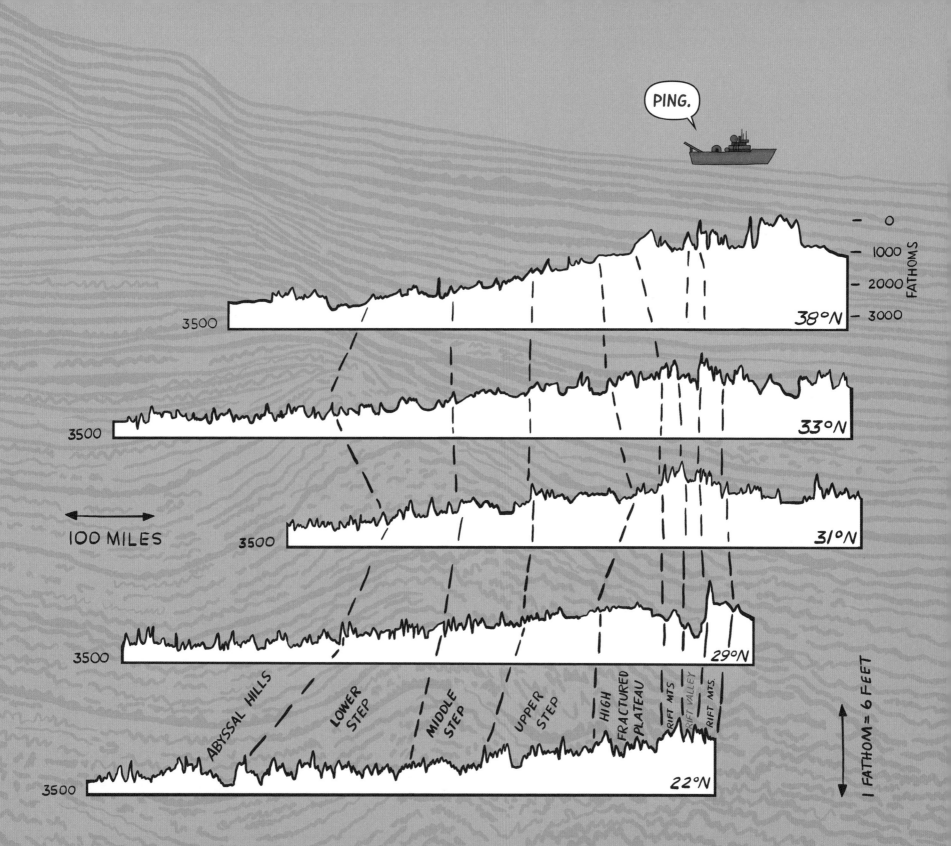

Is this really what it looks like at the bottom of the sea, Miss Tharp? Are there really mountains?

Yes. There are mountains and valleys and plains just like you see on land. For most of history, on maps of the world, the ocean was flat, featureless, and unchanging.

The *World Ocean Floor* panorama is the first map ever made that shows this underwater landscape.

And you made it?

I did.

I am an oceanographic cartographer. I mapped all the oceans in the world.

Like many great stories, Marie's began with curiosity.

Sailors were very superstitious. Their job was dangerous. They lacked scientific knowledge of the oceans and the weather, and their voyages often lasted for months. It was believed that women on board distracted the men and kept them from their duties, which angered the sea gods, who in turn created rough seas. Amid these concerns about securing smooth sailing, the belief grew that women were bad luck aboard merchant and military ships.

Huh?

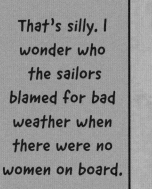

That's silly. I wonder who the sailors blamed for bad weather when there were no women on board.

Women are not responsible for the weather— I am! I'm a cumulonimbus cloud. I can produce heavy rain, and if I try really hard—sometimes hail. Wherever I am, gusty winds are not far behind.

Too bad the sailors did not know about you.

I tried to tell them, but they just wouldn't listen.

In the 1800s women were not allowed aboard these working vessels, yet the myth prevailed that female figureheads carved of wood had the power to calm stormy seas and their eyes could find the way when ships were lost.

The wooden version of me has navigational capabilities. The real version of me is bad luck. I am more useful as an object.

In the early 1900s, women were still considered bad luck aboard ships even after science had disproved the myths.

Sometimes it's hard to convince people to believe something new.

Pangaea is Greek for "all" and "Earth."

Dr. Wegener theorized that Pangaea broke up into the seven continents.

Great idea.

Thank you, Marie. I think so, too.

It took a long time for this change to happen. Dr. Wegener called his theory continental drift.

I like to discover new things.

So did Dr. Alfred Wegener, a German explorer and meteorologist. In 1915, Wegener's book *The Origins of Continents and Oceans* was published. He wrote that a super-continent called Pangaea existed about 250 million years ago.

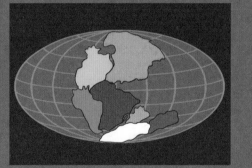

250 million years ago

200 million years ago

100 million years ago

TODAY!

Wegener found the same plant and animal fossils on the different continents. For example, he found fossils of the fern *Glossopteris* in Africa, South America, India, Antarctica, and Australia.

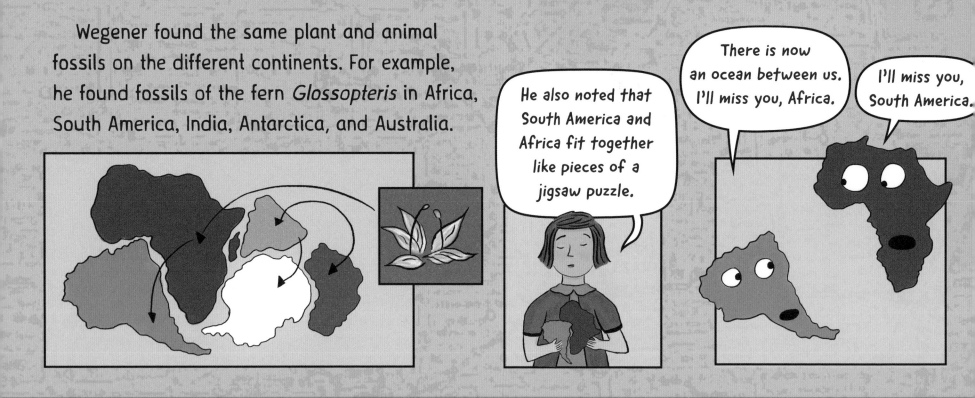

Sadly, not everyone believed him. The scientific community shunned him for his radical ideas.

I first started work as a scientist with my papa. His name was William.

My mama taught German and Latin. Her name was Bertha.

We went all over the country with Papa. He collected samples for soil survey maps for the United States Department of Agriculture.

I was very curious.

Mama and Papa and I traveled light. All we needed was one another.

I asked a lot of questions.

We were constantly on the move. Papa worked in the southern states in the winter and the northern states in the summer. I attended nearly two dozen different schools. It was hard to make friends. I had no sisters and brothers. I was often lonely.

I learned that the world was a big place to discover.

How far away are the stars?

How far away is the moon?

How far away is the ocean?

Very, very far, Marie.

The first time I saw the sea, I was with my mother in Mississippi. It was the most amazing thing I had ever seen. It was constantly moving, just like my family.

I wonder what is underneath all that water, Mama.

I do, too, Marie.

It is just you and me and the great big ocean, Marie.

A few years later we moved to Bellefontaine, Ohio. Papa and Mama bought a farmhouse.

Finally, we have a home.

No more moving around.

We all loved it.

A year later my mama died.

My heart tore and created a rift deep and long that would never heal.

I did not know what I wanted to do with my life. Mama and Papa wanted me to go to college. There were not many career choices for women, and most colleges didn't even admit female students.

How I long to be little again when Mama and Papa and I would travel together, and Mama and I would take long walks.

Papa always told me, "When you find your life's work, make sure it is something that you like to do."

With those words flowing through my broken heart, I left our home in Bellefontaine to study at Ohio University in the fall of 1939.

I was used to going from one place to the other but never before had I gone alone.

I shall miss you very much, Marie.

Goodbye, Papa.

At college, I took classes that were considered "good" classes for women. I began my studies with art, music, English, education, and philosophy.

I took a class in typing, and one in nursing, which was a very popular career for women.

Then I took a course in geology! We discussed volcanoes, fossils, floods, and earthquakes.

I took a class in drafting.

I learned about topography and how to draw a contour map. I became very good at seeing the world in three dimensions on two-dimensional paper.

Then I got really lucky.

One day on the campus bulletin board, I saw an inspiring poster.

At that time most men were off fighting in World War II, and women were needed to do the jobs the soldiers left behind.

Next to the "WOW" poster was a flyer. The University of Michigan offered degrees in petroleum geology. In the 1940s, not many science programs were open to women.

I finished up my classes and graduated with bachelor's degrees in English and music.

In January of 1943 I arrived in Ann Arbor, Michigan, to begin my geology studies. It was very cold.

Looks like I am off to a great start.

I was a studious Petroleum Geology Girl.

I learned about the different kinds of rocks—igneous, metamorphic, and sedimentary—and how they were formed.

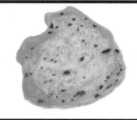

Some were smooth like glass, some had holes like Swiss cheese, some were sparkly like the rocks I found as a child, and others contained fossils.

I read a lot of books on a subject called geomorphology, which is the study of how the landscapes on Earth's surface have been formed by air, water, and ice. Once my class visited Devils Tower in Wyoming.

Any guesses as to how this mass of igneous rock, otherwise known as Devils Tower, was formed?

I believe lava pushed up through the layers of underground sedimentary rock. As it cooled it formed columns. After millions of years, water and wind eroded the softer surrounding rock and the Tower was revealed.

In 1945, I graduated from the University of Michigan with a master's degree in geology and headed to Tulsa, Oklahoma, to work for Stanolind Oil. I was ready to make great discoveries.

The reality was very different.

Do you need any help in the field today?

Sorry, Marie. Your job is here in the office.

I was bored. Papa had said that I should have a job that I liked. I decided to make a change.

I earned good money at Stanolind Oil, so I could afford to take evening classes at the University of Tulsa. I worked really hard and earned a bachelor's degree in math.

Now I was ready to search for something more challenging. I packed my bags and moved to New York City to look for a new job. The year was 1948.

If I can make it there, I can make it anywhere.

Oklahoma

New York

Most of Manhattan is set up like a grid, so it was easy to find Columbia University.

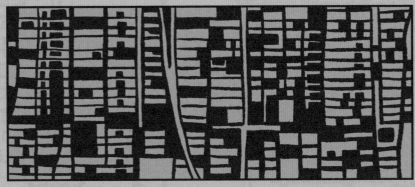

The geologists worked in Schermerhorn Hall. The inscription above the door read,

FOR THE ADVANCEMENT OF
NATURAL SCIENCE
SPEAK TO THE EARTH
AND IT SHALL TEACH THEE

I did not get to speak to the Earth that day, but I did get to speak to the geophysicist Doc Ewing. He had a sea of papers upon his desk.

Tell me about yourself, young lady.

I babbled on and on. I told him about my childhood travels and all the different schools I attended. I told him that I had a bachelor's in math and a master's in geology. And Doc Ewing had just one question . . .

Can you draft?

Yes, I can.

You're hired.

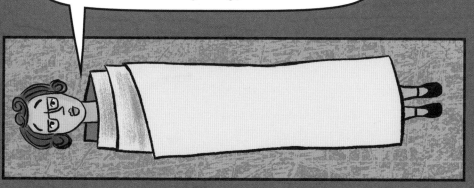

For a heartbeat I felt like a geologist. Unfortunately, I was once again rolled up like a map in office duties. I was hired as an assistant, a human computer, and a copy machine. I wasn't able to assist in research or data collecting. My job had little to do with geology.

There was no topography. There was no geomorphology. There were no fossils.

There were no volcanoes.

When will I get the chance to speak to Earth?

One day, there was a knock at my door.

Bruce had just returned from an expedition on board the ship *Atlantis*.

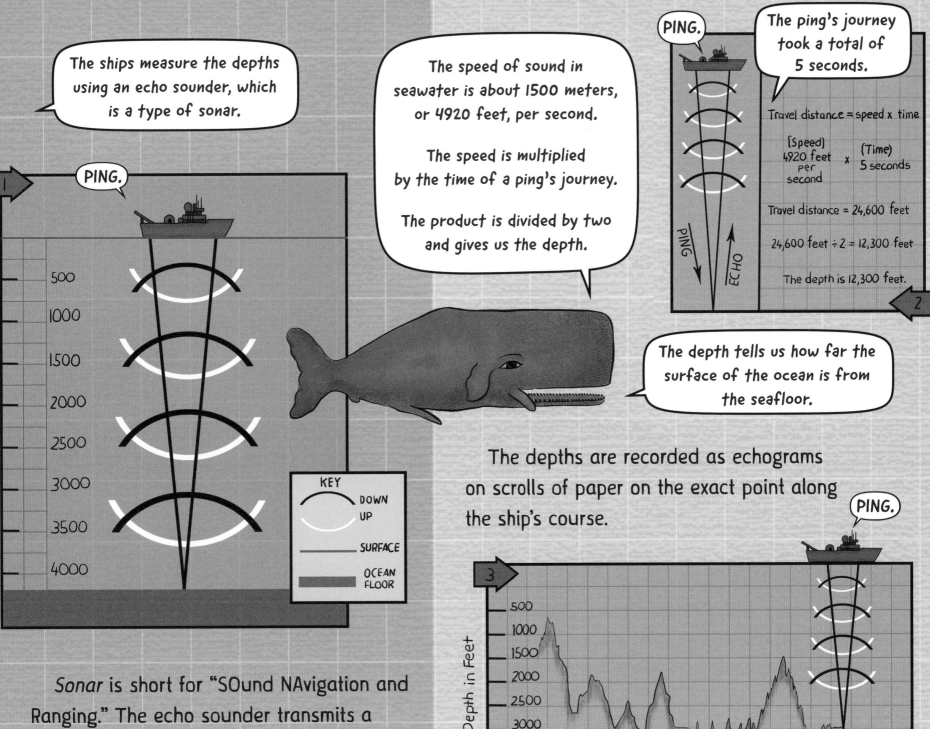

The ships' tracks, or footprints, crossed the Atlantic Ocean like a web made by a very confused spider.

I matched the depths recorded on the echograms to the location of each ship along its track.

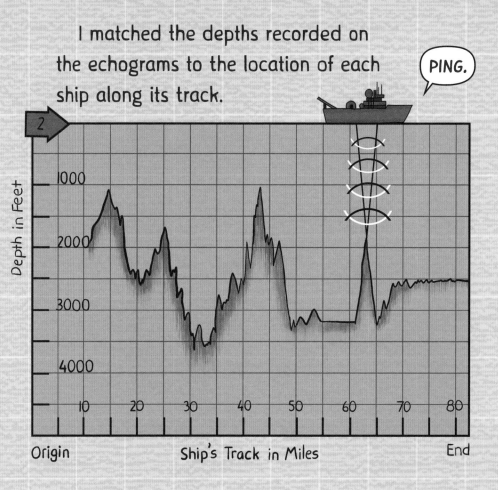

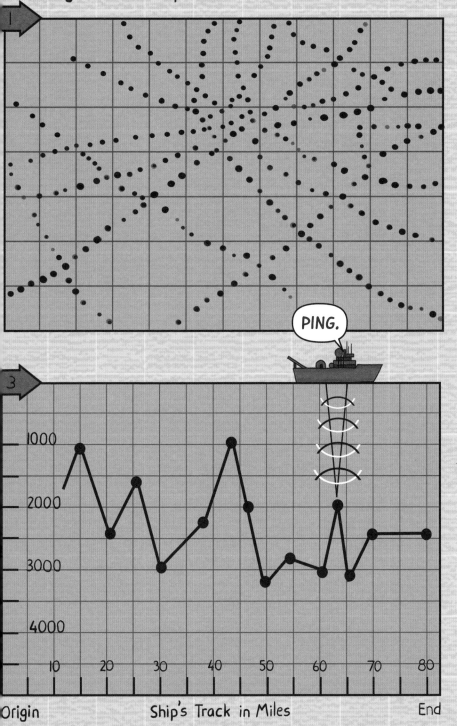

For example: If at 30 miles the sonar ping measured 3000 feet, I put down a dot. If at 63 miles it measured 2000 feet, I put down a dot, and so on. There were thousands of pings, and putting it all together became a challenging game of connect the dots.

Then I arranged the plots of the ships' zigzagging tracks into six straight tracks that crossed the Atlantic Ocean from west to east.

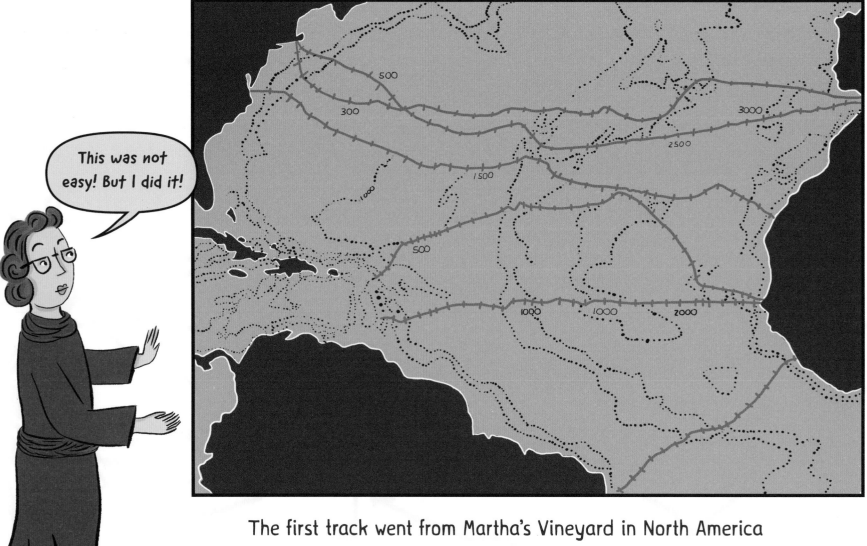

The first track went from Martha's Vineyard in North America to Gibraltar between Europe and Africa over the North Atlantic, with a distance of about 3500 miles.

The last track went from Recife, Brazil, in South America to Freetown, Sierra Leone, in Africa over the South Atlantic, with a distance of almost 2000 miles.

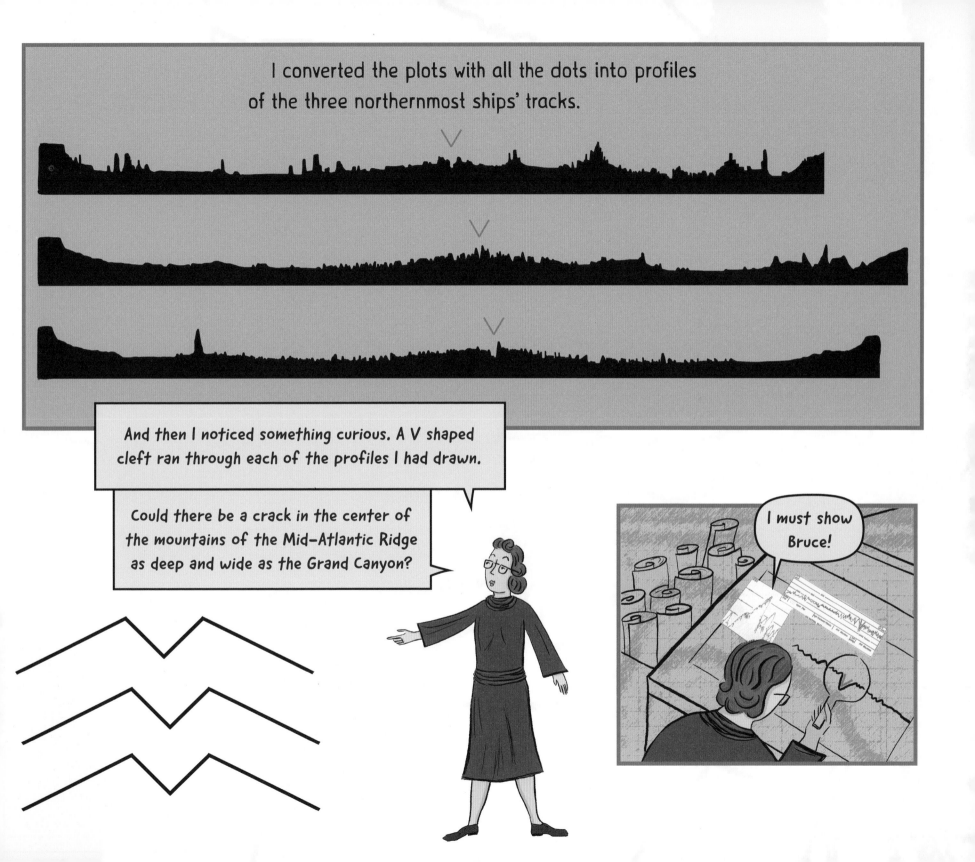

Bruce sailed off to collect more data. Since I was not allowed aboard a research ship, I went back to my drafting tables, piles of paper, and pen and ink. I felt like an ocean whose surface alone could be seen.

Undaunted, I continued to piece together my underwater puzzle. I plotted the southern tracks of the ships between South America and Africa.

There's that V shape again! Let's see what Bruce has to say about this!

I showed Bruce the six notches in the six profiles, from north to south in the Atlantic Ocean.

This is a valley, not "girl talk," Bruce.

You expect me to believe that this rift valley demonstrates the possibility that one continent separated into seven continents as Wegener suggested!

Yes, Bruce.

It would also mean that there is the possibility that the seafloor is spreading and the continents are still moving.

Yes. Correct.

This is scientific heresy!

Perhaps it is the plain old truth.

Bruce instructed me to make a physiographic diagram of the Mid-Atlantic Ridge and the rift valley that traveled down the middle. This kind of map shows the underwater terrain of the Atlantic Ocean as it would look to a soaring bird after all the water had been removed.

As Bruce sent in more data, I added more details. If data were missing, I used my knowledge of geomorphology to fill in the gaps. Slowly, a pattern of this undersea terrain began to emerge.

And then, out of the blue, something happened to help prove the existence of a Mid-Atlantic Rift Valley. Bell Laboratories asked Bruce to map the locations where undersea transatlantic telephone and telegraph cables had broken. If earthquakes were responsible for the breaks, Bell would need to choose other paths, otherwise people wouldn't be able to make telephone calls. Bruce hired a gentleman by the name of Howard Foster to plot the locations of earthquakes. One day I looked over at Howard's desk and saw something amazing.

I placed my physiographic diagram over Howard's map. The light table illuminated them.

Bruce could clearly see that the earthquake epicenters along the Mid-Atlantic Ridge were located within my rift valley.

Bruce and I stared at the red dots snaking along the ridge. It was the one time in my life that I felt Earth move, for it had revealed a secret to me almost too big to comprehend.

The rift is where the magma rises. It cools when it meets the icy seawater and causes earthquakes to occur along the Mid-Atlantic Ridge as Earth's crust forms into the seafloor's mountains and valleys.

Marie, the earthquake data suggest that your rift valley circles the globe like the seam of a baseball. You have discovered the largest geologic feature on Earth. You have convinced me. Now we have to convince the world.

Over the next four years, I worked diligently on my physiographic diagram. I drained the Atlantic Ocean of its billions of gallons of salty water and filled it with a never-before-seen mountainous beauty.

As anticipated, the rift, which split the ocean floor,
once again split the scientific community.

Wegener was a fool.

Wegener was a visionary!

Continents don't move.

If they don't move, how did the valley get there?

Even the famous ocean explorer Jacques Cousteau was so skeptical that he made a film of the North Atlantic, hoping to prove me wrong. It was shown at the first International Oceanographic Congress in 1959 in New York.

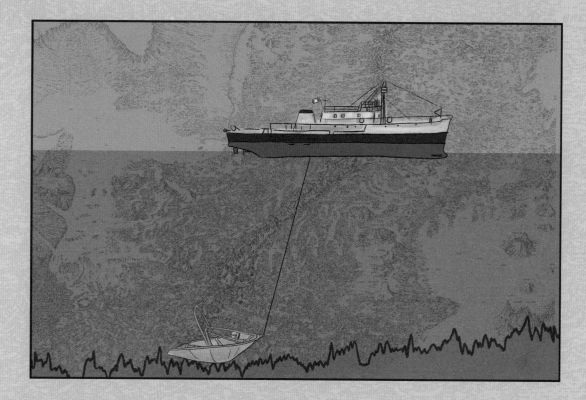

There, in the darkness of the room, Bruce and I got our first real look at the rift valley. On the screen for all to see were the great black cliffs, sprinkled with white glob ooze, which loomed up through the blue-green water.
Bruce, there it is—the Mid-Atlantic Ridge and Rift Valley for all to see.
Jacques Cousteau has proven you right.

Excellent film, Mr. Cousteau. It will do a great deal to support the existence of the rift valley depicted in my profiles.
You are very clever, Miss Tharp. I used your physiographic diagram to plot the tracks of my research ship. I towed my underwater camera, Troika, across the Mid-Atlantic Ocean floor, where you mapped the location of your rift valley and voilà!

Thereafter, scientists' and the public's opinion of the rift valley and Wegener's theory of continental drift slowly began to shift. Opinion also began to change regarding women at sea. In 1965, after fifteen years of working at my desk, Bruce offered me my first spot as a woman aboard a research vessel.

I observed the echo sounder pumping waves of sound to the seafloor. I could hear the whirring of the engines.

My heart beat loudly. The boat gently rocked, and the immensity of the water and its power humbled me.

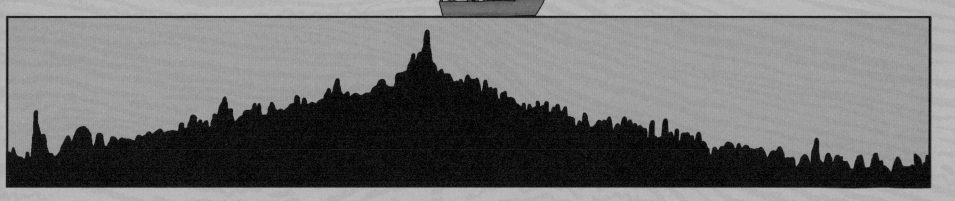

Distant memories floated to the surface of my consciousness. I thought of my papa, now gone, and when he taught me to drive a car at the age of eleven.

I thought of my mama and the first time I had seen the ocean. I remembered paying close attention so that I could find our way home.

In my mind I could clearly see my mother's beautiful face. I could see Papa clearly, too. I could feel them with me.

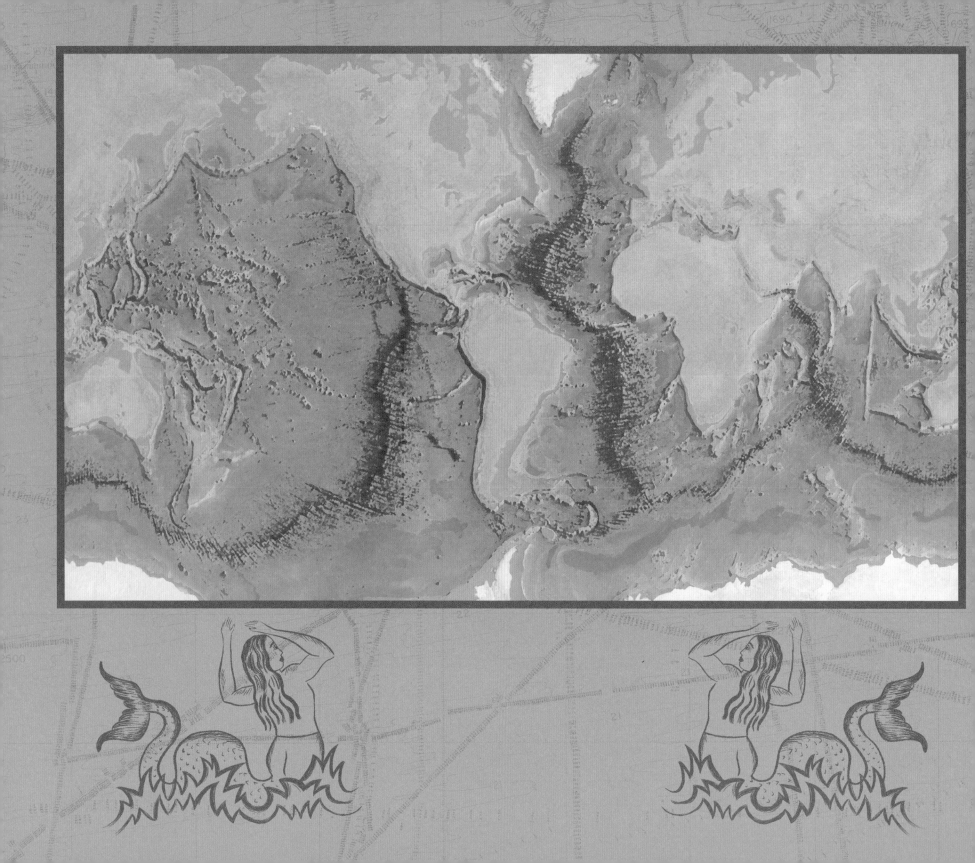

Over many years, Bruce and I mapped all the world's oceans: the Atlantic, Arctic, Indian, Pacific, and the area around Antarctica known as the Southern Ocean. The Austrian landscape artist Heinrich Berann brought my black-and-white ink drawings to life in full color in *National Geographic* magazine and revealed the Mid-Atlantic Ridge and Rift Valley to millions of people around the world. Heinrich, Bruce, and I continued to collaborate and produced an elaborate painting called the *World Ocean Floor* panorama in 1977. This glorious map depicts a one-world ocean whose hidden mountains and valleys, created by the immense forces of Earth, erupted off the canvas and dispersed the idea of a flat and featureless seafloor.

My map of the ocean floor revolutionized the world of geological thinking. It changed scientists' views of Wegener's theory of continental drift and pushed forward the development of the unifying theory of plate tectonics.

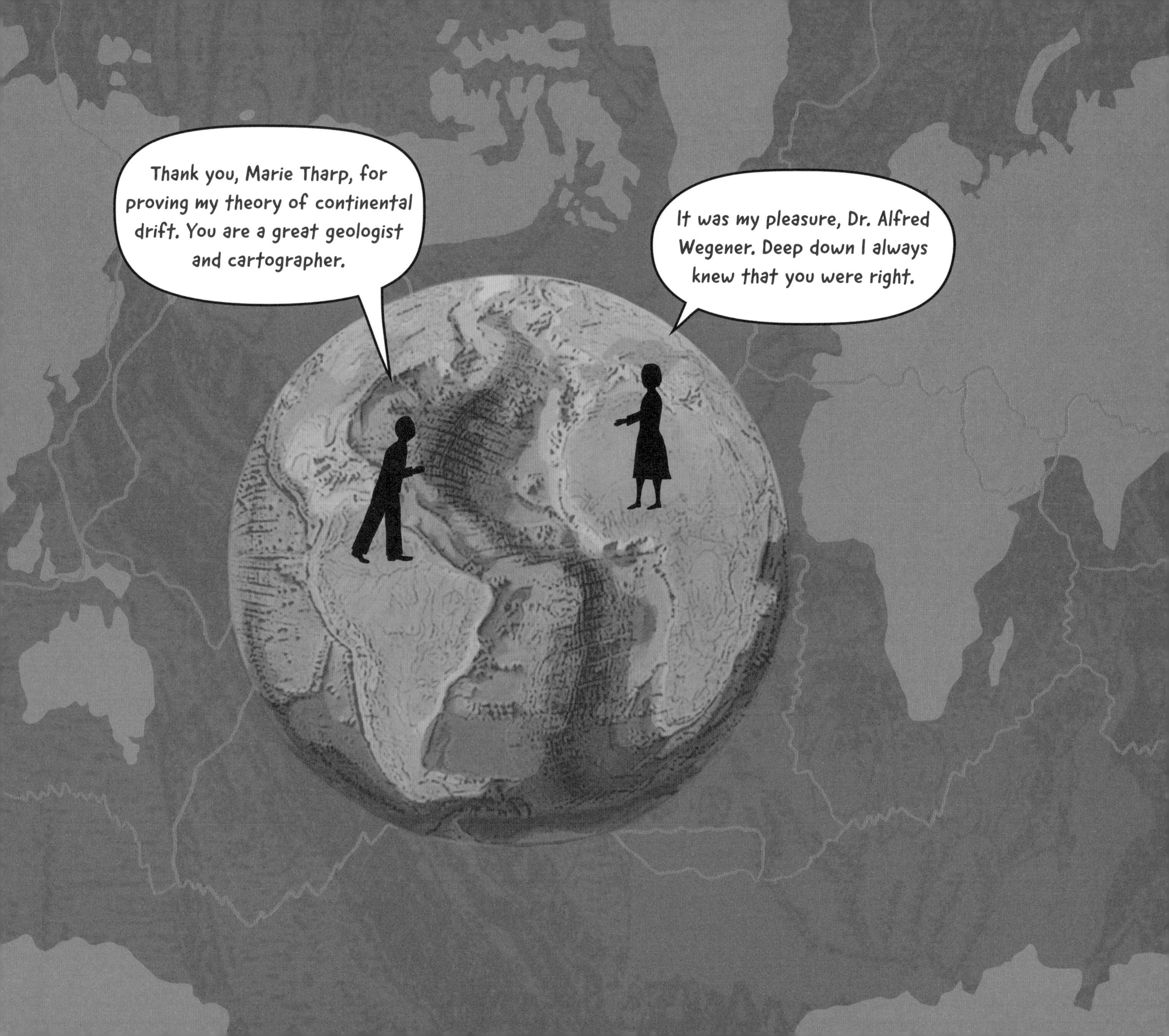
Thank you, Marie Tharp, for proving my theory of continental drift. You are a great geologist and cartographer.
It was my pleasure, Dr. Alfred Wegener. Deep down I always knew that you were right.

AUTHOR'S AFTERWORD

For hundreds of years, men sailed the seas to measure the ocean depths with poles, lead weights, and sonar, but it took a woman named Marie Tharp, born in 1920 in Ypsilanti, Michigan, to shed light on a hidden world thousands of feet under the sea, which started a scientific revolution.

When Marie first mentioned the idea of a rift valley, her colleague Bruce Heezen dismissed her discovery as "girl talk." It would have been easier for Marie to believe that her findings really were just "girl talk." She didn't. She persisted. Marie's creative nature and ability as a spatial thinker allowed her to imagine a seafloor full of plains, valleys, mountains, and deep rifts where the once-huge continent Pangaea had torn apart hundreds of millions of years ago and drifted across Earth's surface. She formed new thoughts and ideas—much like Earth is constantly creating new seafloor—and confronted what was scientifically accepted. Eventually, other scientists opened their eyes to Marie Tharp's ocean.

Throughout her career, Marie mapped all the oceans of the world without the aid of computers and present-day satellite technology. In 1977 she created the first-ever complete map of the ocean floor, the *World Ocean Floor* panorama, with the Austrian landscape painter Heinrich Berann. That same year, Bruce Heezen died unexpectedly, and Marie's life changed drastically. She continued to work at Lamont Geological Observatory, but without Heezen her role was diminished and she retired early in 1982. Thereafter, she received little work as a cartographer and managed to earn a little money with a small map-distribution business, which she ran from her home.

Marie's accomplishments were like the horizon, becoming less visible the farther one sails out to sea, and eventually her name became obscured from the very discovery she made.

After many long years of being in the shadows, Tharp's astounding accomplishments were finally recognized by the Society of Woman Geographers in 1996 with an Outstanding Achievement Award. The Library of Congress then named her one of the four greatest cartographers of the twentieth century in 1997, and the Woods Hole Oceanographic Institution presented Marie with the Mary Sears Women Pioneers in Oceanography Award in 1999. Columbia University and the Lamont-Doherty Earth Observatory awarded the eighty-one-year-old Tharp the first-ever Heritage Award for her life's work as a pioneer of oceanography in 2001.

Marie Tharp died at the age of eighty-six.

Lamont-Doherty

"I had a blank canvas to fill with extraordinary possibilities, a fascinating jigsaw puzzle to piece together. . . . It was a once-in-a-lifetime—a once-in-the-history-of-the-world—opportunity for anyone, but especially for a woman in the 1940s."

"I was so busy making maps I let them argue. I figured I'd show them a picture of where the rift valley was and where it pulled apart. There's truth to the old cliché that a picture is worth a thousand words and that seeing is believing."

—Marie Tharp, 1920–2006

SELECTED BIBLIOGRAPHY

Earth Institute, The Columbia University. "Remembered: Marie Tharp, Pioneering Mapmaker of the Ocean Floor." August 24, 2006. earth.columbia.edu/articles/view/924.

Felt, Hali. *Soundings: The Story of the Remarkable Woman Who Mapped the Ocean Floor.* New York: Picador, Henry Holt & Company, 2012.

Frankel, Henry and Marie Tharp. "Mappers of the Deep: How Two Geologists Plotted the Mid-Atlantic Ridge and Made a Discovery that Revolutionized the Earth Sciences." *Natural History* 95, no. 10 (1986): 49–62.

Heezen, Bruce, Marie Tharp, and Maurice Ewing. "The Floors of the Oceans." The Geological Society of America, Special Paper 65, New York, April 11, 1959. gutenberg.org/files/49069/49069-h/49069-h.htm.

Lawrence, David M. *Upheaval from the Abyss: Ocean Floor Mapping and the Earth Science Revolution.* New Brunswick, NJ: Rutgers University Press, 2002.

Tharp, Marie. "Marie Tharp: Sessions I–IV." By Ronald Doel and Tanya Levin. *Oral History Interviews*, Niels Bohr Library & Archives, American Institute of Physics, 1995–1997. org/history-programs/niels –bohr-library/oral-histories/22896-1.

Wertenbaker, William. *The Floor of the Sea: Maurice Ewing and the Search to Understand the Earth.* Little, Brown: New York, 1974.

Woods Hole Oceanographic Institution. "Marie Tharp Bio." Mary Sears Women Pioneers in Oceanography Award. Excerpt from "Connect the Dots: Mapping the Seafloor and Discovering the Mid-Ocean Ridge" by Marie Tharp, Chapter 2. whoi.edu/sbl/liteSite.do? litesiteid=9092& articleId=13407. Updated December 12, 2006.

Yount, Lisa. *Modern Marine Science: Exploring the Deep.* New York: Chelsea House Publications, 2006.

SOURCE NOTES

"When you find your life's work . . .": Woods Hole Oceanographic Institution, "Marie Tharp Bio."

"girl talk": Wertenbaker, *The Floor of the Sea.*

"There in the darkness . . .": *Oral History Interviews Sessions* I–IV

"I had a blank canvas to fill . . .": The Earth Institute, "Remembered: Marie Tharp."

"I was so busy making maps . . .": The Earth Institute, "Remembered: Marie Tharp."

Most of the backgrounds I created for this book are based on Marie Tharp's original works:

Pages 2, 3, 28, 29, and 31: Reference: "The Floors of the Ocean" by Marie Tharp, Bruce Heezen, and Maurice Ewing.

Pages 4 and 42: My illustration is based upon Heinrich Berann's original painting.

Page 26: I reworked Marie Tharp's original physiographic diagram of the Atlantic Ocean.

Pages 29 and 31: The V shapes marking the location of the Mid-Atlantic Rift Valley are approximations within one hundred kilometers of where Marie Tharp first indentified the notches in her six original profiles.

Page 40: This illustration is based upon a NOAA satellite image, which I used as a reference. oceanservice.noaa.gov.

Steve Sagala

Henry Holt and Company, *Publishers since 1866*
Henry Holt® is a registered trademark of Macmillan Publishing Group, LLC
120 Broadway, New York, NY 10271 • mackids.com

Copyright © 2020 by JoAnn Adinolfi
All rights reserved
Library of Congress Control Number: 2020904449
ISBN 978-1-250-21473-7

Our books may be purchased in bulk for promotional, educational, or business use.
Please contact your local bookseller or the Macmillan Corporate and Premium Sales Department at
(800) 221-7945 ext. 5442 or by email at MacmillanSpecialMarkets@macmillan.com.

First edition, 2020

Designed by Vera Soki and Angela Jun
The artist used Adobe Photoshop and collage to create the illustrations for this book.
Printed in China by Toppan Leefung Printing Ltd., Dongguan City, Guangdong Province

1 3 5 7 9 10 8 6 4 2